50 Easy Soup Recipes

(50 Easy Soup Recipes - Volume 1)

Joy Gonzalez

Copyright: Published in the United States by Joy Gonzalez/ © JOY GONZALEZ

Published on November, 19 2020

All rights reserved. No part of this publication may be reproduced, stored in retrieval system, copied in any form or by any means, electronic, mechanical, photocopying, recording or otherwise transmitted without written permission from the publisher. Please do not participate in or encourage piracy of this material in any way. You must not circulate this book in any format. JOY GONZALEZ does not control or direct users' actions and is not responsible for the information or content shared, harm and/or actions of the book readers.

In accordance with the U.S. Copyright Act of 1976, the scanning, uploading and electronic sharing of any part of this book without the permission of the publisher constitute unlawful piracy and theft of the author's intellectual property. If you would like to use material from the book (other than just simply for reviewing the book), prior permission must be obtained by contacting the author at author@chardrecipes.com

Thank you for your support of the author's rights.

Content

50 AWESOME EASY SOUP RECIPES 4

1. All In One Soup Dumpling Recipe............. 4
2. Carrot, Cashew And Coconut Soup Recipe 4
3. Chai Roasted Pumpkin Soup With Honey Walnuts Recipe 5
4. Chicken Noodle Soup With Vegetables Recipe 5
5. Chicken And Pearl Barley Soup Recipe 6
6. Chicken, Corn And Ginger Soup With Bacon Recipe 6
7. Chinese Chicken And Sweet Corn Soup Recipe 6
8. Cinnamon Spiced Lamb Soup With Pearl Couscous Recipe.. 7
9. Coconut Chicken Soup Recipe 7
10. Creamy Mushroom Soup Recipe................ 8
11. Curried Lentil And Vegetable Soup Recipe 8
12. Curried Pumpkin Soup With Ginger 9
13. Easy Beef And Vegetable Soup Recipe....... 9
14. Easy Pea And Ham Soup............................ 9
15. Easy Vegetable Soup 10
16. French Onion Soup Mix Recipe................ 10
17. Greek Style Egg, Lemon And Chicken Soup Recipe 10
18. Green Soup With Olive Oil And Kale Chips Recipe 11
19. Maltese Lentil Soup.................................. 11
20. Matzo Ball Chicken Noodle Soup Recipe 12
21. Meatball, Zucchini And Chickpea Soup Recipe 12
22. Mexican Tomato Soup 13
23. Potato Goulash Soup Recipe 13
24. Potato And Leek Soup 14
25. Pumpkin Miso Soup Recipe 14
26. Pumpkin And Split Pea Soup Recipe 15
27. Quick Chicken And Sweet Corn Soup...... 15
28. Roast Cauliflower Dhal Soup Recipe 16
29. Roast Pumpkin Soup Easy Recipe 16
30. Roasted Broccoli And Almond Soup Recipe 17
31. Rustic Bean Soup 17
32. Simple Curried Pumpkin Soup Recipe 17
33. Slow Cooker Chicken And Winter Vegetable Soup Recipe 18
34. Slow Cooker Pea And Ham Soup Recipe . 18
35. Spanish Bacon And Vegetable Soup Recipe 19
36. Spanish Rice Soup Recipe 19
37. Spicy Chorizo Soup Recipe........................ 19
38. Spicy Lentil Soup Recipe............................ 20
39. Spicy Zucchini And Fennel Soup Recipe .. 20
40. Super Simple Roast Pumpkin Soup Recipe 21
41. TIFFXO: Tiffiny Hall's Moroccan Lamb And Chickpea Soup Recipe 21
42. Thai Chicken Noodle Soup 22
43. Thai Pumpkin Soup 22
44. Thai Style Sweet Potato Soup Recipe 22
45. Tomato, Chilli And Coriander Soup Recipe 23
46. Tuscan Bean Soup Recipe........................... 23
47. Vegetarian Greek Lentil Soup Recipe......... 24
48. Vietnamese Style Chicken Noodle Soup Recipes.. 24
49. White Bean Soup With Chorizo Soup 25
50. Winter Warmer Pumpkin And Turmeric Soup Recipe 25

INDEX 26
CONCLUSION 28

50 Awesome Easy Soup Recipes

***

1. All In One Soup Dumpling Recipe

Serving: 0 | Prep: 45mins | Cook: 30mins | Ready in: 75mins

Ingredients

- 1 L Massel* chicken stock (liquid)
- Dough
- 400 g plain flour
- 1/2 cup hot water
- Jelly stock
- 1/2 tbs gelatine
- 1 cup Massel* chicken stock (liquid)
- Filling
- 10 leaves Chinese cabbage blanched
- 500 g pork mince
- 2 sprigs spring onions
- 1/2 tsp minced ginger
- 1 tbs soy sauce
- 1 tsp sesame oil
- 10 water chestnuts

Direction

- Add half a cup of Massel chicken stock with half a tablespoon of gelatine. Put in the fridge till it becomes a jelly like consistency
- Put flour and hot water into food processor and process to a ball. Tip on to board and knead for 10 minutes till shiny. Wrap in cling wrap and leave aside for half an hour.
- Chop 2 pieces of the cabbage and add to a mixing bowl, then add the remaining filling ingredients, but leave the other eight pieces of cabbage.
- Take a small bowl out and line with cling wrap. Line it with the cabbage leaves, and leave the sides overhanging. Divide the mixed pork mixture into 4. Take a portion of the pork mixture and put it into the cabbage lined bowl. Fold the cabbage over the pork mixture. Gather the cling wrap and twist securely at the top. Repeat steps for the remaining three portions as above. Put in fridge.
- Heat a steamer to steam dumplings.
- Remove dough from cling wrap and divide into 4 portions. Flatten each portion to a size of a bread plate. Take the pork mixture from the fridge, unwrap it and then place in the centre of the dough. Gather the dough at the top and press the top of the dough together to secure the pork mixture.
- Put dumplings in a steamer for 15 minutes. Next, heat the stock.
- Get a bowl and take the dumpling out of steamer and place into a bowl. Pour some stock over the dumpling and garnish with coriander before serving.

2. Carrot, Cashew And Coconut Soup Recipe

Serving: 1 | Prep: 8mins | Cook: 35mins | Ready in: 43mins

Ingredients

- 1 tbs unsalted butter
- 4 carrots chopped peeled
- 1 onion chopped
- 1/2 cup Massel* Vegetable Liquid Stock
- 1/2 cup coconut milk
- 1 tbs cashew paste
- 2 sprigs fresh parsley
- 1/2 egg hard-boiled
- 1 pinch salt *to taste

- 1 pinch pepper *to taste

Direction

- Melt butter in a saucepan over medium heat. Add carrots, onion, salt, pepper and stir until the carrots have softened.
- Then add coconut milk and cashew paste. Bring it to a boil and reduce the heat, then let it cook for 20 minutes.
- Let the soup cool slightly, puree with a stick blender until smooth. Slowly thin with water to bring the desired consistency.
- Garnish with fresh parsley leaves and boiled egg (add eyes and carrot wings to make it a baby chick) and serve hot.

3. Chai Roasted Pumpkin Soup With Honey Walnuts Recipe

Serving: 2 | Prep: 15mins | Cook: 45mins | Ready in: 60mins

Ingredients

- 1kg pumpkin coarsely chopped
- 1/2 tsp cardamom ground
- 1/4 tsp cinnamon ground
- 1/2 tsp freshly ground black pepper
- 1 spray olive oil
- 1/4 cup walnuts
- 1 tsp honey
- 2 tsp rice bran oil
- 1 onion small coarsely chopped
- 2 garlic cloves sliced
- 3/4 cup vegetable stock (liquid)
- 1 3/4 cups water
- 1/3 cup low-fat Greek yoghurt
- 2 tbs coriander coarsely chopped

Direction

- Preheat oven to 200C. Line a large oven tray with baking paper.
- Place pumpkin on the tray in a single layer. Sprinkle with cardamom, cinnamon and pepper, then spray with oil.
- Roast for 25 minutes or until tender.
- Meanwhile, line a small oven tray with baking paper. Place nuts on tray and then drizzle with honey. Roast for 5 minutes or until golden. Cool.
- Heat rice bran oil in a large saucepan over medium heat. Cook onion and garlic, stirring, for 5 minutes or until softened.
- Add pumpkin, stock and the water to the pan, then bring to the boil. Remove from heat and cool for 10 minutes.
- Blend or process pumpkin mixture until smooth. Return pan to the heat and stir until hot.
- To serve, drizzle soup with yoghurt, a sprinkle of honey nuts and coriander.

4. Chicken Noodle Soup With Vegetables Recipe

Serving: 6 | Prep: 10mins | Cook: 20mins | Ready in: 30mins

Ingredients

- 1 chicken breast fillet, cubed
- 1 brown onion, diced
- 90g Home Brand chicken noodle instant soup
- 2 carrots, finely diced
- 3 cups frozen mixed vegetables, finely diced
- 8 cups water

Direction

- Combine the chicken noodle soup with 8 cups of boiling water in a saucepan. Return to the boil.
- Add remaining ingredients and reduce heat to simmer.
- Simmer until chicken has turned white and vegetables are tender, approximately 20 minutes.

- Taste soup and add another 1-2 cups of water if desired.
- Serve with crusty hot bread.

5. Chicken And Pearl Barley Soup Recipe

Serving: 4 | Prep: 15mins | Cook: 60mins | Ready in: 75mins

Ingredients

- 1/2 chicken
- 1 onion chopped
- 1 leek cleaned sliced
- 2 carrots peeled sliced
- 1 fennel bulb finely chopped
- 2 garlic cloves crushed
- 1 tbs parsley fresh *to decorate
- 2 sprigs thyme
- 1 bay leaf
- 1 1/2 cups pearl barley
- 1 tbs chicken stock powder
- 1 pinch black pepper
- 2 celery sticks
- 3 L water

Direction

- Add chicken, onion, leek, carrots, fennel, celery, garlic, thyme sprigs, bay leaf, chicken stock powder and water to a large pot. Cover with lid, and bring to boil, then reduce the heat and simmer until the meat is soft and easy come off from the bones (Don't forget remove the scum).
- Transfer the meat into a bowl, leave to cool, then remove from bones and cut to smaller pieces.
- Add barley into soup and cook until soft. Use tongs to remove thyme sprigs and bay leaf. Return the meat back into soup, stir taste and season with salt and pepper.
- Serve the soup hot on it's own or with fresh bread roll and garnish with parsley.

6. Chicken, Corn And Ginger Soup With Bacon Recipe

Serving: 4 | Prep: 30mins | Cook: 70mins | Ready in: 100mins

Ingredients

- 1 tbs butter
- 2 celery sticks diced
- 1 onion diced
- 4 garlic cloves peeled small finely diced
- 2 bacon rashers diced rindless
- 1 ginger finely grated peeled
- 2 tsp curry powder
- 3 cups cooked chicken shredded
- 425 g canned corn cob kernels
- 425 g cream-style canned corn
- 3/4 cup pearl barley
- 5 cups Massel* Chicken Style Liquid Stock
- 1 tbs cornflour
- 1/2 tsp salt and pepper *to taste

Direction

- Heat butter in a pan, add onion, garlic, celery, ginger, bacon and curry powder.
- Cook until soft and aromatic, then transfer to a saucepan and add chicken, corn kernels, creamed corn, chicken stock, barley and salt and pepper.
- Cook on a low heat for approximately 1 hour. Add more stock if desired or cornflour combined with water to create desired consistency.

7. Chinese Chicken And Sweet Corn Soup Recipe

Serving: 6 | Prep: 10mins | Cook: 20mins | Ready in: 30mins

Ingredients

- 1 leek cleaned white part only finely diced
- 1 tbs vegetable oil
- 4 cups Massel* Chicken Style Liquid Stock
- 1 whole BBQ chicken
- 425 g canned creamed corn
- 2 eggs lightly beaten
- 3 spring onions finely sliced

Direction

- Cut all the white meat from the barbecue chicken. Remove the skin and then cut the meat into small bite-sized pieces. Set aside.
- Heat the vegetable oil in a large saucepan over a medium heat. Add leek and cook until translucent.
- Add the chicken stock and bring to the boil. Turn down heat to a simmer then add the chicken pieces and the creamed corn.
- Stir through and allow to simmer for 20 minutes.
- Take off heat and using a fork, gently stir the soup as you add the beaten egg in a continuous stream. Continue stirring the soup with the fork for another minute once all the egg has been added.
- Serve immediately with a small handful of chopped spring onions as a garnish.

8. Cinnamon Spiced Lamb Soup With Pearl Couscous Recipe

Serving: 6 | Prep: 20mins | Cook: 145mins | Ready in: 165mins

Ingredients

- 4 lamb shanks trimmed
- 1 tbs olive oil
- 1 onion diced
- 2 carrots diced
- 1 stalk celery diced
- 1/2 tsp allspice
- 400 g tomato puree
- 1 1/2 L vegetable stock (liquid)
- 1 cup pearl couscous
- 1 lemon chopped juiced
- 1 handful parsley *to serve
- 1 tsp ground cinnamon

Direction

- Heat a large heavy-based saucepan over a moderately high heat. Seal the lamb shanks in the oil for 8 minutes or until well coloured, then set them aside.
- Add the onion, carrot and celery and cook for 3 minutes. Add the spices and stir for 30 seconds. Place the shanks back in, add tomato puree and stock. Bring to the boil, cover and turn down to a gentle simmer. Cook for 2 hours or until the meat is very tender. Take the pan off the stove.
- Remove the shanks and set aside until cool enough to handle. Pull the meat off the bone and shred it with forks.
- Set the soup over a moderate heat and add the shredded meat and couscous. Cook for 10-15 minutes or until the couscous is cooked. Season with salt and pepper. Add lemon juice to taste, sprinkle with chopped parsley and serve.

9. Coconut Chicken Soup Recipe

Serving: 4 | Prep: 10mins | Cook: 25mins | Ready in: 35mins

Ingredients

- 1 L Campbell's Real Thai Soup Base
- 500 g chicken thighs
- 2 carrots
- 2 zucchinis
- 4 leaves silverbeet
- 400 g canned coconut cream
- 250 g rice noodles
- 2 tbs oil

Direction

- Slice the chicken thinly, and cut carrots and zucchini into matchsticks. Finely slice silverbeet leaves. Place rice noodles into hot water to soften.
- Heat oil in a large saucepan and fry chicken thighs for 3 minutes. Pour in soup base, then bring to the boil and let simmer for about 12-15 minutes.
- Add in carrots, zucchini, silverbeet and rice noodles and allow to simmer for about 5 minutes.
- Pour in coconut cream. Stir to combine, then serve.

10. Creamy Mushroom Soup Recipe

Serving: 4 | Prep: 20mins | Cook: 30mins | Ready in: 50mins

Ingredients

- 1 large brown onion, diced
- Olive or vegetable oil
- 6 large big potatoes, peeled and cut into small pieces
- 1/2 teaspoon caraway seeds, ground
- 3 large bay leaves
- Whole mushrooms (230 g in jar), sliced
- 500 g fresh button mushrooms button, peeled then sliced
- 1 heap tbsp of fresh dill, chopped
- 300 ml thickened cream
- Vegeta gourmet stock seasoning
- 4 boiled eggs
- Salt
- Black pepper
- 2 tbsp cornflour mixed with a little water

Direction

- Heat little oil in a large saucepan over medium heat. Add onion and cook until translucent.
- Add caraway seeds stir then add potatoes, bay leaves and slowly pour in about 2L boiling water.
- Cover with lid and simmer until the potatoes start soften then add both mushrooms. Cook until the mushrooms are soft.
- Pick out the bay leaves. Add thickened cream, dill and slowly pour in cornflour mixed with little water. Keep stirring and cook until bubbling and the soup thickens.
- Taste and season with Vegeta, salt and pepper.
- Serve on a plate and top with halved cooked egg.

11. Curried Lentil And Vegetable Soup Recipe

Serving: 4 | Prep: 20mins | Cook: 40mins | Ready in: 60mins

Ingredients

- 1 tbs olive oil
- 3 garlic cloves crushed
- 1 onion diced
- 1 ginger grated
- 3 carrots diced
- 1 parsnip diced
- 1/2 green capsicum chopped
- 2 long red chillies thinly sliced
- 3 celery sticks diced
- 200g red lentils rinsed
- 2 tsp curry powder
- 1/2 tsp fennel seeds
- 2 tsp cumin seeds
- 1 tsp black pepper *to taste
- 1 1/2L reduced-salt vegetable stock (liquid)

Direction

- Saute garlic, ginger and onion in hot oil until onion is transparent.
- Add carrots, celery, capsicum and chillies, saute until slightly tender.

- Add spices and cook for several minutes until fragrant.
- Add lentils and stock, cook for approximately 30 minutes, adding more stock or water if too thick.

12. Curried Pumpkin Soup With Ginger

Serving: 4 | Prep: 15mins | Cook: 30mins | Ready in: 45mins

Ingredients

- 1 tbs olive oil
- 1 onion chopped
- 2 tbs fresh ginger grated
- 2 garlic cloves minced
- 1 tbs Indian curry powder
- 4 cups pumpkin cubed
- 1 carrot medium sliced
- 4 cups Massel* Vegetable Liquid Stock
- 1 pinch salt and pepper *to taste
- 1/2 cup low-fat cooking cream
- Curry blend
- 1 tbs ground coriander
- 1 tbs ground cumin
- 1 tsp paprika
- 1 tsp ground turmeric
- 1 tsp chilli powder
- 1 tsp salt

Direction

- Heat oil in a large saucepan, then fry onions, garlic and ginger until onion is transparent.
- Add curry blend and cook for 1-2 minutes.
- Add pumpkin and carrot, and fry for 2-3 minutes, stirring, to coat with onion mixture.
- Add stock to cover and cook until vegetables are soft.
- Allow to cool.
- Place in a blender with cream and blend until smooth.

13. Easy Beef And Vegetable Soup Recipe

Serving: 6 | Prep: 20mins | Cook: 120mins | Ready in: 140mins

Ingredients

- 500g gravy beef chopped
- 1/2 cup pearl barley washed
- 2 onions
- 3 potatoes
- 2 carrots
- 3 celery sticks
- 1/2 turnip
- 4 cups water
- 3 beef stock cubes
- 1 pinch salt and pepper
- 1/2 swede

Direction

- Chop all vegetables.
- Put all ingredients in a saucepan and add enough water to just cover.
- Simmer gently for a couple of hours until beef is tender.

14. Easy Pea And Ham Soup

Serving: 4 | Prep: 10mins | Cook: 120mins | Ready in: 130mins

Ingredients

- 1 water
- 1 cup onion chopped
- 1 tsp vegetable oil
- 500 g dried split peas
- 500 g bacon bones
- 1 seasoning

Direction

- In a large pot, sauté onions in oil. Add split peas and ham bone. Add enough water to cover ingredient and season with salt and pepper.
- Cover, and cook for 2 hours until there are no peas left, just a green liquid. While it is cooking, check to see if water has evaporated. You may need to add more water as the soup continues to cook.
- Once the soup is a green liquid remove from heat, and let stand so it will thicken. Once thickened you may need to heat through to serve.

15. Easy Vegetable Soup

Serving: 0 | Prep: 45mins | Cook: 0S | Ready in: 45mins

Ingredients

- 3 brown onions
- 5 stalks celery
- 1 large sweet potato
- 2 parsnips
- 1 turnip
- 4 carrots
- 2 tablespoons butter
- 3 L water
- 1/4 cup good quality vegetable stock powder
- 1/2 bunch fresh coriander

Direction

- Add butter into a large saucepan.
- Peel and chop all vegetables into small, even sizes and add to saucepan.
- Sweat vegetables over a medium heat for approximately 5 minutes, stirring occasionally.
- Dissolve stock powder in hot water and add to vegetables.
- Chop up coriander and add to saucepan. Bring to a boil, boil for approximately 25 minutes until vegetables are cooked.
- Ladle ⅔ of the vegetables back into a large heatproof jug and puree with a stab blender or food processor. Return puree to saucepan.

16. French Onion Soup Mix Recipe

Serving: 4 | Prep: 15mins | Cook: 0S | Ready in: 15mins

Ingredients

- 3/4 cup dried onion minced
- 4 1/2 tbs Massel* Beef Stock Powder
- 4 tsp onion powder
- 1/4 tsp celery seed crushed
- 1/4 tsp sugar
- 1/4 tsp curry powder *to taste
- 1 pinch white pepper

Direction

- Mix and store in an airtight container.

17. Greek Style Egg, Lemon And Chicken Soup Recipe

Serving: 6 | Prep: 10mins | Cook: 20mins | Ready in: 30mins

Ingredients

- 1 1/2 cups risoni pasta
- 3 L chicken stock (liquid)
- 4 eggs
- 2 lemons small
- 2 bay leaves
- 500 g chicken thighs
- 2 cups silverbeet chopped
- 1 splash olive oil
- 1 handful parsley oil chopped *to serve

Direction

- Place stock in a pot and bring to the boil. Add risoni and cook for 5-6 minutes.
- Beat eggs together in a separate bowl. Add the lemon juice from the two small lemons and whisk together. Set aside.
- Reduce heat until stock stops boiling. Take a half cup measure of stock, careful not to scoop any risoni, and pour into egg mixture, whisking to combine. The mixture should remain smooth without any scrambled pieces of eggs.
- Add another ½ cup of stock to the eggs and whisk, repeating 3-4 times.
- Then pour egg mixture back into pot with risoni and stir. Simmer for 5 or so minutes, being careful to not boil it.
- Add silverbeet. Simmer for 10-15 minutes until soup thickens stirring occasionally. Remove bay leaves.
- In the meantime, place a drizzle of olive oil and chicken thighs into a pan and cook until golden brown, turning as needed. Set aside and slice.
- Once soup is thickened, serve and place some shredded chicken on top of each bowl with a generous amount of chopped parsley.

18. Green Soup With Olive Oil And Kale Chips Recipe

Serving: 10 | Prep: 15mins | Cook: 30mins | Ready in: 45mins

Ingredients

- 2 fennel bulbs white bulb roughly chopped
- 3 leeks whites roughly chopped
- 1 bunch kale
- 2 brown onions peeled roughly chopped
- 1 parmesan rind
- 1 parsley pod *optional
- A pinch salt and pepper *to taste
- 2 - 2.5L Massel* Chicken Style Liquid Stock
- A splash extra virgin olive oil

Direction

- In a large pot with a lid turn on Medium heat and add the fennel, leek, onions, parmesan, salt and pepper. Sweat down for 5 minutes and add the stock.
- Cook with the lid on until tender. Add 2/3 of the kale and parsley for 5 minutes. Let cool for 15 minutes. Remove parmesan rind.
- Blend until smooth.
- Meanwhile to make the kale chips, place kale on a baking tray. Drizzle with olive oil, salt and bake for 8-10 minutes until crunchy.
- Serve with a good drizzle of extra virgin olive oil, salt, and kale chips

19. Maltese Lentil Soup

Serving: 6 | Prep: 10mins | Cook: 40mins | Ready in: 50mins

Ingredients

- 200 g red lentils
- 500ml Massel* Vegetable Liquid Stock
- 500 ml tomato juice
- 400 g canned chopped tomato
- 1 red onion chopped large
- 2 carrot large thinly sliced
- 2 celery stick finely chopped
- 2 garlic clove crushed
- 1 tbs canola oil

Direction

- Heat oil in a large saucepan and add the chopped onion. Cook until softened but not coloured.
- Stir in the celery, garlic and carrots and cook for a further 5 minutes.
- Add the juice, chopped tomatoes and stock to the pot and then pour in the dried lentils, stirring to combine.

- Increase heat, bring to the boil, then reduce heat to low and simmer gently, covered, for approximately 30 minutes.
- Allow to cool slightly, then blend the soup, adding a little water or stock if mixture is too thick.

20. Matzo Ball Chicken Noodle Soup Recipe

Serving: 2 | Prep: 15mins | Cook: 90mins | Ready in: 105mins

Ingredients

- 1 packet Slendier spaghetti
- 2 chicken Maryland pieces skinless
- 2 celery sticks diced large
- 2 carrots diced large
- 2 parsnips diced medium
- 1 1/2 L water
- 1/2 red onion cut into wedges
- 1 1/2 tsp garlic powder
- 1 handful parsley chopped fresh
- Matzo balls
- 2 slices wholemeal bread
- 1/4 tsp baking powder
- 1/2 tsp garlic powder
- 1 pinch pepper
- 1 egg lightly beaten
- 1 tsp vegetable oil

Direction

- Prepare Slendier spaghetti as per instructions on the back of the pack.
- Heat a large stock pot over a high heat. Add chicken in two batches. Cook for 2 minutes on each side, or until golden
- Add all chicken to the pot with ½ carrot, ½ celery, ½ parsnips, onion and garlic powder. Bring to the boil, then simmer for about 40 minutes, or until chicken is starting to fall from the bone.
- Remove the chicken. Cool and shred meat discarding the bones. Reserve cooking liquid.
- To make the matzo balls: pulse bread in a food processor until mixture resembles breadcrumbs. Combine with baking powder and garlic powder in a bowl. Season with pepper, then stir in combined egg and oil with a fork.
- Refrigerate, covered until firm. Roll tablespoons of mixture into balls. Place on a plate and refrigerate again.
- Strain cooking liquid into a large clean stock pot. Add remaining carrot, celery and parsnips, and bring to the boil, then reduce to a simmer and add the matzo balls.
- Simmer covered for 20 minutes. Add spaghetti and chicken. Cook for 5 minutes, or until the matzo balls are cooked through. Garnish with fresh parsley.

21. Meatball, Zucchini And Chickpea Soup Recipe

Serving: 4 | Prep: 10mins | Cook: 20mins | Ready in: 30mins

Ingredients

- 500 g lean beef mince
- 2 garlic cloves crushed
- 1 red onion finely chopped small
- 1/2 cup panko breadcrumbs
- 2 tbs fresh basil leaves finely chopped
- 1 handful fresh basil leaves *to serve *extra
- 1 egg lightly beaten
- 700 g passata
- 1 1/2 L salt-reduced beef stock
- 2 cups water
- 400 g canned chickpeas drained rinsed
- 2 zucchinis cut into 1cm cubes
- 60 g baby spinach leaves
- 1 handful parmesan shaved *to serve
- 4 slices wholegrain bread *to serve
- 1 olive oil *to serve

- 1 pinch salt and pepper *to taste

Direction

- In a large bowl, combine mince, garlic, onion, breadcrumbs, basil and egg. Season and combine well. Roll heaped tablespoons of mince mixture into balls and place on a large plate.
- In a large saucepan, add passata, stock and 2 cups of water. Cover and bring to the boil over high heat. Reduce heat to medium and simmer, uncovered, for 5 minutes. Add meatballs and cook for 5 minutes. Add chickpeas and zucchini and cook for a further 2-3 minutes. Remove from heat and stir through baby spinach. Season with salt and pepper.
- Ladle soup into bowls and sprinkle with extra basil and parmesan. Serve with bread drizzled with a little olive oil.

22. Mexican Tomato Soup

Serving: 0 | Prep: 0S | Cook: 60mins | Ready in: 60mins

Ingredients

- 2 tbs olive oil
- 2 onion chopped
- 3 garlic clove chopped
- 3 tsp Mexican seasoning
- 1 tsp smoked paprika
- 800 g canned chopped tomato
- 6 cups Massel* Beef Style Liquid Stock
- 1/3 cup tomato paste
- 1 1/2 cup red lentils
- 2 tbs brown sugar
- 1/3 cup fresh coriander chopped

Direction

- In a large saucepan, heat the oil and add onions and garlic. Cook until light golden.
- Mix in the Mexican seasoning and smoked paprika.
- Add tomatoes, stock, tomato paste, lentils and sugar.
- Bring to the boil, stir, then reduce heat and simmer for 45 minutes.
- Add chopped fresh coriander just before serving.
- Serve with sour cream, extra chopped coriander and cheesy scones.

23. Potato Goulash Soup Recipe

Serving: 6 | Prep: 10mins | Cook: 20mins | Ready in: 30mins

Ingredients

- 6 potatoes large peeled cut into chunks
- 2 carrots large sliced
- 1 brown onion
- 2 tbs olive oil
- 1 tsp caraway seeds ground
- 4 garlic cloves crushed
- 2 tbs smoky paprika
- 1 tbs dried marjoram crushed
- 1 pinch salt *to taste
- 1 pinch pepper *to taste
- 150 g oyster mushrooms chopped
- 3 kransky sausages diced
- 3/4 cup spring onions sliced
- 1 tbs Massel* Beef Stock Powder
- 3 tbs cornflour
- 150 ml water

Direction

- Mix water and cornflour together.
- Heat oil in deep saucepan over medium heat. Add onion and carrots and cook until the colour is released from carrots.
- Add potatoes, caraway seeds and garlic. Cook for 2 minutes. Add paprika, stir and cook for 1 minute.

- Pour in enough water to cover the potatoes. Bring the soup to boil, then reduce the heat and simmer until the potatoes and carrots are soft.
- Heat another frying pan over medium heat. Add slices of Kransky sausages and cook until golden brown then add to soup.
- Add the mushrooms, marjoram, beef stock powder, shallots and season with salt and pepper. Stir.
- If you prefer the soup thicker, add cornflour mixed with water and cook until bubbling.
- Serve on its own or with fresh bread rolls.

24. Potato And Leek Soup

Serving: 8 | Prep: 15mins | Cook: 45mins | Ready in: 60mins

Ingredients

- 2 leek sliced
- 4 potato diced large
- 1L Massel* Chicken Style Liquid Stock
- 1 tbs butter
- 200 ml cream

Direction

- Place leeks in a large pot with butter and cook until transparent.
- Then add potatoes and cook for 4-5 minutes.
- Add chicken stock, reduce heat and allow to simmer for approximately 30 minutes or until potatoes are very soft.
- Remove from heat and using a stick blender, blend until smooth.
- Add cream and stir thoroughly.

25. Pumpkin Miso Soup Recipe

Serving: 0 | Prep: 15mins | Cook: 60mins | Ready in: 75mins

Ingredients

- 1/2 jap pumpkin skin off
- 2 onions finely sliced
- 3 garlic cloves crushed
- 1/4 cup olive oil
- 1 L vegetable stock (liquid)
- 1/4 cup white miso paste
- 1 hemp oil
- 1 can chickpeas drained patted dry with paper towel
- 1/2 cup pomegranate, seeds removed
- 200 g Brussels sprouts halved
- 2 tbs vegetable oil
- 1 pinch salt and pepper
- Hemp pesto
- 2 cups kale torn leaves only
- 1/2 bunch basil
- 1/4 cup almonds
- 1 garlic clove
- 1/2 cup Hemp Foods Australia hemp oil
- 3 tbs Hemp Foods Australia hemp seeds
- 1 pinch salt *to taste

Direction

- For the soup, pour the oil into a large saucepan. Cut the pumpkin into small pieces and add to the pan with the onion and garlic. Season with a little salt and cook over a medium heat for 25 minutes covered with a lid, stirring frequently to sweat and soften the vegetables.
- Once the vegetables have softened, add the stock and miso, and continue to cook until the pumpkin is very soft, for approximately 10 minutes.
- Puree the soup in an upright blender, or with a hand held blender. Return to the pot, season and set aside until ready to serve.
- Preheat the oven to 190C. Separately toss the Brussels sprouts and chickpeas in the oil and

seasoning, and bake on separate trays lined with baking paper for 15 minutes, or until golden and crispy. The chickpeas may need longer to get crispy.
- To make the hemp pesto: combine hemp pesto ingredients to a food processor and blitz to a paste.
- Reheat the soup, adjust consistency with a little water if needed, adjust seasoning and serve topped with hemp pesto, roasted Brussels sprouts, chickpeas and pomegranate. Drizzle with a little hemp oil if desired.

26. Pumpkin And Split Pea Soup Recipe

Serving: 4 | Prep: 20mins | Cook: 45mins | Ready in: 65mins

Ingredients

- 290 g split peas soaked overnight
- 600 g pumpkin cubed
- 1 onion chopped
- 4 tomatoes cubed skin off
- 1 bunch fresh coriander chopped
- 1 fresh green chilli thinly sliced
- 1 1/2 tsp dried tarragon
- 1 tsp ground turmeric
- 1/2 tsp ground cumin
- 1 tbs Nuttelex margarine
- 3/4 cup coconut cream
- 1 Massel* vegetable stock cube
- 1 mango cubed
- 1 tsp coconut sugar
- 1 pinch sea salt

Direction

- In a large pot of 1.5L water cook soaked chickpeas.
- When ready, melt 1 generous tbsp of margarine in a big pot and add your onion to saute. Add the pumpkin and fry for approx 5 minutes. Stir occasionally
- Skin the tomatoes. Best is to cut little crosses on the bottom and put into hot water for one minute. Remove the skin and cut into cubes. Add to the pot with the coriander, chili, herbs and spices. Stir well, fry for a minute and turn down the heat to middle heat.
- Now add the complete split pea pot into your pumpkin pot. You probably will need to add a bit more water. Add the stock cube and stir well. Let it simmer for about 10 minutes.
- Now finish the soup. Add the coconut cream and mango. Stir well and give it another low simmer for approx 15 minutes. Then have a taste. Give the soup a rest of 15 minutes. As longer it gets a rest, as better the taste. When ready plate up, garnish with some watercress.

27. Quick Chicken And Sweet Corn Soup

Serving: 4 | Prep: 0S | Cook: 15mins | Ready in: 15mins

Ingredients

- 45 g chicken noodle instant soup
- 880 g cream-style canned corn
- 4 spring onions chopped
- 2 eggs lightly beaten
- 4 cups water

Direction

- Cook soup with water as per directions.
- Add creamed corn. Simmer very gently for 5 minutes.
- Remove from heat.
- Slowly pour in lightly beaten eggs, stirring with fork.
- Add spring onions and serve.

28. Roast Cauliflower Dhal Soup Recipe

Serving: 6 | Prep: 15mins | Cook: 40mins | Ready in: 55mins

Ingredients

- 1 cauliflower cut into florets
- 2 tbs ghee melted
- 1L Massel* Vegetable Liquid Stock
- 500 ml water
- 210 g red lentils
- 1 brown onion finely chopped large
- 4 garlic cloves crushed
- 3 tsp ground turmeric
- 1 red chilli finely chopped
- Tarka
- 2 tbs ghee melted
- 1 tsp cumin seeds
- 1 tsp black mustard seeds
- 12 fresh curry leaves
- 1 brown onion large quartered sliced lengthways
- 2 garlic cloves crushed
- 1 red chilli sliced
- 1 lemon rind zested
- 1 tub natural yoghurt
- 1 packet roti bread *to serve

Direction

- Preheat oven to 220C or 200C fan forced. Line a baking tray with paper. Place cauliflower on prepared tray. Drizzle with ghee and season with salt and pepper. Toss to coat. Roast for 20-25 minutes, or until edges turn brown
- Meanwhile, place the Massel Liquid Vegetable Stock and water in a saucepan over high heat. Add lentils. Bring to the boil. Skim and discard foam. Stir in onion, garlic, ginger, turmeric and chilli. Season. Simmer, stirring occasionally for 30-35 minutes, or until lentils break down
- Remove from heat and add roasted cauliflower. Blend with a hand held mixer until smooth.
- For the tarka: heat ghee in a frying pan over medium heat. Add cumin, mustard seeds and cook, stirring for 1 minute or until aromatic. Add curry leaves, cook for 30 seconds or until aromatic. Add onion and cook, stirring for 4-5 minutes until golden. Add garlic, chilli and rind and cook, stirring for 2 minutes or until aromatic.
- Reserve a third cup of mixture. Add the remaining tarka mix and 2tbs lemon juice to the cauliflower mixture. Cook stirring for 2-3 minutes or until warmed through. Season well.
- Ladle soup among bowls. Top with reserved tarka mix. Serve with yoghurt and pan-fried roti bread.

29. Roast Pumpkin Soup Easy Recipe

Serving: 4 | Prep: 10mins | Cook: 60mins | Ready in: 70mins

Ingredients

- 750 g pumpkin cubed peeled seeded
- 2 carrots coarsely chopped
- 2 onions cut into wedges
- 1 garlic clove peeled
- 2 1/2 tbs olive oil
- 1 potato diced large
- 1 L water
- 4 tsp chicken stock powder
- 1 cup cream
- 1 tsp ground nutmeg
- 1 pinch salt and pepper *to taste

Direction

- Preheat oven to 180C.
- Place pumpkin, carrots, onions and garlic in a baking dish or roasting pan.
- Drizzle with olive oil and bake for 40-60 minutes until soft.

- In a large pot over medium heat, bring water and chicken stock to a boil. Cook potato in simmering water until soft.
- Combine potato and water with roasted vegetables and puree in a blender or food processor, or by using a stick mixer until smooth.
- Return to pot over low heat and stir in cream, nutmeg, pepper and salt. Heat gently before serving.

30. Roasted Broccoli And Almond Soup Recipe

Serving: 4 | Prep: 15mins | Cook: 35mins | Ready in: 50mins

Ingredients

- 4 garlic cloves peeled whole
- 2 tbs extra virgin olive oil
- 2 tsp chilli dried
- 6 pieces soy and linseed bread
- 2 cups broccoli roasted
- 1/2 cup almonds roasted
- 250 g cannellini beans drained rinsed
- 2 tbs lemon juice
- 1 1/2 L chicken stock (liquid) good quality
- 1 handful parsley fresh *to garnish

Direction

- Preheat the oven to 180C - 200C and on an oven tray place the broccoli, garlic, olive oil and chilli, then cook for 10 - 15 minutes. Let the mixture cool for 10 minutes.
- In a food processor, add all of the ingredients including the broccoli tray ingredients, except for the stock, and blend until smooth.
- Place the mixture into a saucepan with the stock and cook over a low heat for 10 minutes.
- Serve with crusty soy and linseed bread and fresh parsley.

31. Rustic Bean Soup

Serving: 2 | Prep: 10mins | Cook: 35mins | Ready in: 45mins

Ingredients

- 400 g canned mixed beans
- 1 onion diced
- 1 potato cut in half peeled
- 1 tbs tomato paste
- 400 g water
- 3 tbs olive oil
- 1/3 cup pasta
- 1/3 cup parsley chopped
- 1 pinch salt and pepper
- 1 pinch chilli flakes *optional

Direction

- In a large saucepan, fry diced onion in olive oil. Add potato and cook for 1 minute. Add tomato paste, can of beans and water.
- Bring to boil. Add the dried pasta of your choice. Simmer till pasta has cooked through.
- Break up cooked potato with fork so broth of soup thickens.
- Season with salt and pepper, and maybe some chilli flakes (optional).
- When ready to serve, fold through chopped parsley.

32. Simple Curried Pumpkin Soup Recipe

Serving: 4 | Prep: 20mins | Cook: 40mins | Ready in: 60mins

Ingredients

- 1 tbs oil
- 1 onion diced medium
- 2 tsp McCormick garlic powder

- 3 tbs KEEN'S Traditional Curry Powder
- 1 potato large peeled cut into 2cm cubes
- 1 kg pumpkin peeled cut into 2cm cubes
- 1 1/2 L vegetable stock (liquid)
- 120 ml thickened cream

Direction

- Heat the oil in a large saucepan on high. Sauté the onion, garlic and KEEN'S curry powder in the oil until soft.
- Add the potato, pumpkin and stock, then bring to the boil. Simmer for 40 minutes.
- Purée until smooth, then add the cream and season to taste.

33. Slow Cooker Chicken And Winter Vegetable Soup Recipe

Serving: 6 | Prep: 0S | Cook: 185mins | Ready in: 185mins

Ingredients

- 1 turnip medium
- 1 parsnip medium
- 1 onion chopped medium
- 3 carrots large
- 5 celery stalks
- 2 spinach leaves finely chopped large
- 1 red capsicum diced small
- 500 g chicken breast fillet cut into pieces
- 1 sprig fresh thyme
- 2 chicken stock cubes crushed
- 6 cups water
- 2 bay leaves
- 1/4 bunch parsley finely chopped stems trimmed
- 3/4 tsp nutmeg
- 45 g French onion soup mix
- 1 1/2 tbs crushed garlic
- 1 tbs olive oil

Direction

- Place water in slow cooker and turn to high. Add stock cubes, soup mix and salt and pepper to slow cooker and stir.
- Chop turnip, parsnip, carrots and celery into small, even pieces, then add to slow cooker and stir.
- Heat a tablespoon of oil in a fry pan on medium heat and cook the onion and garlic together for 2-3 minutes until they are just starting to turn opaque. Do not brown.
- Add onion and garlic to slow cooker and stir.
- Add parsley and thyme and stir.
- Season the chicken evenly with salt and freshly ground pepper.
- In the same pan used for the onions, cook the chicken in 2-3 small batches until chicken starts to brown.
- Add chicken to the slow cooker including any juices and scrapings from the fry pan. Stir.
- Add nutmeg and bay leaves and stir.
- Cook for 2½ hours.
- Add capsicum and spinach, stir and cook for a further 60 minutes.
- Remove the bay leaves and thyme.
- Taste for any extra seasoning requirements.
- Serve warm.

34. Slow Cooker Pea And Ham Soup Recipe

Serving: 6 | Prep: 15mins | Cook: 480mins | Ready in: 495mins

Ingredients

- 800g ham hock
- 1 brown onion finely diced
- 2 carrots chopped
- 2 celery sticks chopped
- 2 cups yellow split peas rinsed
- 1 bay leaf
- 10 cups water

Direction

- Place split peas on the bottom of a slow cooker.
- Add carrots, celery, onion, bay leaf and ham hock.
- Cover with water.
- Cook on low for 6-8 hours or high for 4-6 hours, or until meat will fall off the bone easily.
- Remove bone, discard fat and skin. Chop meat and return to soup. Stir then serve.

35. Spanish Bacon And Vegetable Soup Recipe

Serving: 6 | Prep: 20mins | Cook: 35mins | Ready in: 55mins

Ingredients

- 1 tbs olive oil
- 2 garlic cloves finely chopped
- 1 onion diced
- 250 g bacon rashers diced
- 2 celery sticks sliced
- 2 carrots diced
- 2 potatoes diced
- 1 broccoli stalk diced
- 1 L Campbell's Real Spanish Soup Base
- 1 can kidney beans
- 1 can black beans
- 1 can chopped tomatoes
- 1/2 cup macaroni
- 1/2 cup brown rice

Direction

- Heat oil in a large saucepan over medium heat, then add bacon, onion, celery, garlic and fry until onion is softened.
- Add canned tomatoes and Campbell's Real Spanish Soup Base, then turn up the heat and bring to the boil.
- Add in all other ingredients, reduce heat and simmer, covered for 30 minutes until veggies are soft and rice is tender.
- Season with salt and pepper. Serve with a dollop of pesto and/or parmesan cheese.

36. Spanish Rice Soup Recipe

Serving: 4 | Prep: 15mins | Cook: 15mins | Ready in: 30mins

Ingredients

- 1 L Campbell's Real Spanish Soup Base
- 1 onion medium sliced strips
- 400 g beef chuck steak, sliced
- 2 potatoes diced medium
- 440 g canned chopped tomatoes
- 1 cup brown jasmine rice
- 150 g chorizo sausage

Direction

- Cook rice in a rice cooker as per directions substituting half a cup of soup base for part of the 2 cups water required.
- While the rice is cooking, brown beef strips in heavy based pan. Remove from pan and keep warm.
- Saute onion strips until transparent, then add can of chopped tomatoes and diced potato. Add remainder of Campbell's Soup Base and the beef. Bring to boil and simmer for 10 minutes until potato is tender.
- Add cooked rice and stir, then simmer for 3 minutes to allow rice to absorb the flavour.
- Serve and enjoy.

37. Spicy Chorizo Soup Recipe

Serving: 4 | Prep: 15mins | Cook: 40mins | Ready in: 55mins

Ingredients

- 1 onion finely chopped

- 1 carrot finely chopped
- 1 stalk celery finely chopped
- 1/2 capsicum finely chopped
- 3 tbs olive oil
- 1 tsp smoked paprika
- 1 tsp ground cumin
- 1 can whole tomatoes
- 400 g chickpeas drained
- 200 g chorizo sausages
- 2 bacon rashers
- 1 tbs light soy sauce
- 1 handful parsley finely chopped
- 700 ml Massel* chicken stock (liquid)

Direction

- Add the olive oil into your largest pot and add finely chopped onion, celery, carrot and capsicum. Saute until brown bits are starting to form then transfer to a plate.
- Add finely diced bacon and sliced chorizo to pot. Saute on medium-high heat until they appear crispy and browned and a reddish oil is appearing in the pot.
- Add vegetables back into pot with the meat and saute with paprika and cumin for 2-3 mins or until the paprika an cumin become aromatic.
- Add stock, tomatoes, chickpeas, soy sauce and simmer for 20 mins. If it looks too thick add some water or more stock.
- After 20 mins turn off heat and allow to cool slightly before serving. Serve with a generous sprinkle of parsley and over-the-top buttered, crusty bread.

38. Spicy Lentil Soup Recipe

Serving: 4 | Prep: 15mins | Cook: 30mins | Ready in: 45mins

Ingredients

- 1 tsp oil
- 1 onion finely diced
- 1 tsp ginger grated
- 1 tsp garlic minced
- 1 tsp ground cumin
- 1 tsp ground coriander
- 1 cup red lentils dried
- 1L Massel* Vegetable Liquid Stock
- 425 g diced tomatoes
- 1 lemon juiced

Direction

- Heat oil in pan, add onion, ginger, garlic, turmeric, cumin and coriander. Cook for a few minutes until fragrant.
- Add lentils and stir to coat. Add stock and tomatoes.
- Bring to the boil then simmer for 25 minutes or until lentils are cooked.
- Stir in lemon juice and serve.

39. Spicy Zucchini And Fennel Soup Recipe

Serving: 4 | Prep: 15mins | Cook: 30mins | Ready in: 45mins

Ingredients

- 3 zucchinis large
- 1 fennel bulb cubed small
- 1 carrot cubed large
- 2 potatoes cubed large skinned
- 1 onion small
- 500ml Massel* Vegetable Liquid Stock
- 1/2 tsp cayenne pepper
- 1/4 tsp sea salt
- 1 splash sunflower oil for frying
- Sour cream mix
- 3 tbs plain yoghurt
- 2 tbs lemon juice
- 1 dash sea salt
- To serve
- 2 tbs fennel leaves chopped

Direction

- Prepare the vegies. Heat some sunflower oil in a pot. Add the onion and fry until slightly golden. Add the carrot and potato. Fry for another 2-3 minutes. Add fennel and fry for further 2 minutes. Stir well.
- Add zucchinis and fry for a further 2 minutes. Deglaze with the vegetable stock. Season with cayenne pepper and sea salt, and bring to the boil for 10 seconds. Turn down the heat and simmer until the vegetables are done.
- When the vegetables are done, turn off the heat and rest until cooled down. When ready, use your hand food processor and process the soup until you achieve a smooth, creamy consistency. If you don't like it creamy, just roughly process.
- Mix the coconut yoghurt with lemon juice and sea salt. Add a tablespoon to the soup when you plate, and sprinkle with some fresh fennel greens.

40. Super Simple Roast Pumpkin Soup Recipe

Serving: 4 | Prep: 15mins | Cook: 45mins | Ready in: 60mins

Ingredients

- 1 butternut pumpkin cubed
- 1 red onion cut into wedges
- 2 garlic cloves
- 1 tbs olive oil
- 750 ml Massel* Chicken Style Liquid Stock
- 1 1/2 tbs honey
- 2 tsp Dijon mustard
- 1 pinch salt and pepper *to taste

Direction

- Preheat oven to 220C.
- Coat cubed pumpkin with oil, garlic and place on roasting tray.
- Scatter onion throughout pumpkin.
- Cook pumpkin and onion for 40 minutes or until golden and caramelised.
- Heat stock and add cooked pumpkin, onion, honey, mustard, pepper and salt.
- Blend until soup has a smooth consistency.

41. TIFFXO: Tiffiny Hall's Moroccan Lamb And Chickpea Soup Recipe

Serving: 2 | Prep: 15mins | Cook: 55mins | Ready in: 70mins

Ingredients

- 2 tsp olive oil
- 300 g lamb shoulder (boneless) cubed trimmed
- 1 pinch salt and pepper *to taste
- 1 onion finely diced
- 1 garlic clove
- 1 tsp ground cumin
- 1 tsp ground coriander
- 2 cups chicken stock (liquid)
- 1 can diced tomatoes
- 1 carrot diced
- 1/2 can chickpeas drained rinsed
- 2 tbs Greek yoghurt *to serve
- 2 sprigs coriander *to serve

Direction

- Heat oil in a large non-stick saucepan over medium-high heat. Season lamb with salt and pepper and cook for 5 minutes until well browned. Remove from pan and set aside.
- In the same pan, add the onion and cook for 5 minutes until translucent. Add the garlic, cumin, coriander and cook for a further 1 minute. Add the chicken stock, tomatoes, carrot and cook for 40-45 minutes until the lamb is tender. Add the chickpeas and cook for 2 minutes to heat through.

- Divide soup among 2 bowls and serve hot with a dollop of Greek yoghurt and top with fresh coriander.

42. Thai Chicken Noodle Soup

Serving: 4 | Prep: 10mins | Cook: 25mins | Ready in: 35mins

Ingredients

- 1 L Campbell's Real Thai Soup Base
- 1 tbs olive oil
- 3 garlic cloves thinly sliced
- 1/2 red capsicum deseeded cut into small pieces
- 1 lemongrass stalk diced
- 2 tsp lime juice
- 400 ml cold water
- 150 g vermicelli
- 1 handful baby spinach fresh
- 1/2 cup coriander fresh
- 400 g barbecue chicken breast cut into small pieces

Direction

- Heat the oil in a large saucepan over medium-high heat, then add the garlic and lemongrass and cook for 1-2 minutes, or until fragrant.
- Add the stock then bring to the boil.
- Then add noodles, lime juice, capsicum and cook until the noodles are cooked (1-2 minutes).
- Then add the water, chicken, coriander and bring to the boil again. Taste the soup and see if anything needs to be added.
- Serve hot on its own and enjoy.

43. Thai Pumpkin Soup

Serving: 6 | Prep: 15mins | Cook: 18mins | Ready in: 33mins

Ingredients

- 1/2 butternut pumpkin chopped
- 1 sweet potato chopped peeled
- 2 carrot chopped peeled
- 1 onion sliced
- 2 potato chopped peeled
- 3 tsp ginger
- 1 tbs lemon juice
- 3 tsp red Thai curry paste
- 1 tsp parsley
- 1 tsp coriander
- 400 ml coconut cream
- 2 cups Massel* Chicken Style Liquid Stock
- 2 tsp pepper
- 1 tsp butter

Direction

- Peel and chop vegetables into large pieces and set aside.
- In a pressure cooker sauté onion and garlic with a teaspoon of butter, then pop in curry paste give it a stir.
- Add all the Vegetables, coconut cream, stock, lemon juice and spices. Give it a mix and pressure cook for 18 minutes.
- Blend and serve with crusty bread

44. Thai Style Sweet Potato Soup Recipe

Serving: 4 | Prep: 0S | Cook: 70mins | Ready in: 70mins

Ingredients

- 2 sweet potatoes large
- 2 onions large
- 2 tbs brown sugar
- 4 tbs peanut oil

- 2 tbs red Thai curry paste
- 3 tbs ginger finely grated
- 2L Massel* Chicken Style Liquid Stock
- 200 ml coconut milk
- 2 cups fresh mixed herbs chopped
- 2 limes juiced

Direction

- Preheat oven to 200C.
- Place sweet potato and onion on a large baking tray.
- Scatter the brown sugar and half the peanut oil over the top and shake the tray to coat the vegetables.
- Bake the vegetables for 45 minutes, turning a few times during cooking.
- Once cooked, the potatoes and onions should be honey brown and caramelised, not black.
- Into a large, deep pot add the remaining oil, curry paste and ginger.
- Cook over a medium heat for about 3 minutes to release the flavours.
- Add cooked vegetables and combine.
- Pour in the stock and simmer for about 15 minutes.
- Blend the mixture until smooth.
- Add the coconut milk, stir through and simmer for 3-5 minutes.
- Add the fresh greens, stir in well and add the lime juice to taste.
- Stir well and serve.

45. Tomato, Chilli And Coriander Soup Recipe

Serving: 4 | Prep: 15mins | Cook: 10mins | Ready in: 25mins

Ingredients

- 10 tomatoes chopped
- 1 onion finely diced
- 2 garlic cloves finely chopped
- 1 red chilli finely chopped
- 1 cup Massel* Vegetable Liquid Stock
- 1/2 tsp salt and pepper optional
- 1 tsp fresh coriander roughly chopped

Direction

- Fry off onions over low-medium heat until softened, then add garlic and chilli, and fry for 1 minute further while stirring.
- Add diced tomatoes, then simmer for 5-10 minutes until softened.
- Remove from heat, add salt and pepper, cool slightly then puree.
- Add warmed stock and combine well.
- Stir through coriander or garnish individual serves with coriander.

46. Tuscan Bean Soup Recipe

Serving: 4 | Prep: 10mins | Cook: 25mins | Ready in: 35mins

Ingredients

- 3 tbs olive oil
- 3 tbs fresh flat-leaf parsley
- 2 tbs oregano
- 1 onion diced
- 1 tbs parmesan cheese
- 2 leeks sliced
- 1 potato diced large
- 2 garlic cloves crushed
- 5 cups Massel* Vegetable Liquid Stock
- 800 g canned butter beans
- 1/4 cabbage shredded

Direction

- Heat oil and cook onion, leek, garlic and potato.
- Pour in stock and liquid from beans and simmer for 15 minutes.
- Stir in beans, shredded cabbage and half of the herbs.

- Season with salt and pepper and simmer for 10 minutes, or until beans are soft.
- Blend the soup and serve garnished with remaining herbs and Parmesan cheese.

47. Vegetarian Greek Lentil Soup Recipe

Serving: 6 | Prep: 20mins | Cook: 60mins | Ready in: 80mins

Ingredients

- 600g brown lentils soaked
- 400g potatoes quartered
- 150g carrot quartered
- 300g zucchini
- 150g celery halved and sliced
- 100g red capsicum quartered
- 150g cherry tomatoes
- 100g onion chopped
- 3 garlic cloves finely chopped
- 2 spring onions sliced
- 2 tbs organic cold pressed extra virgin olive oil
- 1 1/2 tsp pink salt
- 1/2 tsp pepper
- 2 1/5 tsp dried oregano
- 1/2 cinnamon
- 1 tsp smoked paprika
- 2 tbs fresh lemon juice
- 1 bay leaf
- 1/2 tbs maple syrup
- 5 tbs organic passata
- 1.5L filtered water
- Fresh dill to serve
- Fresh parsley to serve

Direction

- Heat olive oil in a big pot and fry the onions until slightly golden. Add potatoes and carrots. Fry for 5 minutes and stir constantly.
- Add zucchini, celery, capsicum, cherry tomatoes, garlic and spring onions and mix well.
- Deglaze with 1.5L of water and add the soaked lentils.
- Bring to the boil and turn down to a simmer. Add the salt, pepper, oregano, cinnamon, paprika, lemon juice, bay leaf, maple syrup and passata.
- Simmer for around 45 minutes or until vegies are tender and turn off the heat.
- Top with fresh dill or parsley and serve.

48. Vietnamese Style Chicken Noodle Soup Recipes

Serving: 4 | Prep: 10mins | Cook: 20mins | Ready in: 30mins

Ingredients

- 250 g vermicelli noodles
- 1 barbecued cooked chicken shredded boneless
- 2 cm ginger cut into matchsticks peeled
- 3 garlic cloves sliced
- 1L Massel* Chicken Style Liquid Stock
- 2 tbs soy sauce
- 1 tbs fish sauce
- 2 tbs hoisin sauce
- 2 tbs sugar
- 1 lime cut into wedges
- 1 bunch coriander leaves roughly chopped
- 1 bunch mint leaves
- 1/2 cup peanuts
- 1 long red chilli sliced *optional

Direction

- In a large saucepan, add in the chicken stock, ginger and garlic and bring to the boil. Once boiling add in the soy sauce, fish sauce, hoisin and sugar. Stir well then add in the vermicelli noodles. Cook the noodles in the broth until they are al dente.

- Next, add the chicken to the stock and stir through, and continue to cook until the chicken heats through.
- Remove the pot from the stove and add in the coriander and mint saving a few herbs for garnishing. Add a squeeze of lime and then serve the soup in bowls.
- Top with extra herbs, a lime wedge and a sprinkle of peanuts and chilli if you like it hot!

49. White Bean Soup With Chorizo Soup

Serving: 6 | Prep: 15mins | Cook: 35mins | Ready in: 50mins

Ingredients

- 1 L Campbell's Real Spanish Soup Base
- 1 L water cold
- 300 g white beans dried
- 250 g Gotzinger cheese kransky
- 2 chorizo sausages
- 5 potatoes large
- 1 tbs dried marjoram heaped
- 1 carrot large
- 6 garlic cloves crushed
- 60 g cornflour
- 1 pinch Vegeta Gourmet Stock vegetable powder
- 1 red onion
- 3/4 cup fresh parsley *to garnish

Direction

- Soak the beans in cold water overnight, then drain and put in a saucepan. Cover with water and place the lid on. Bring to the boil, then reduce the heat and cook until the beans are soft. Drain.
- Pour the Real Soup Base into a large saucepan and add carrot, potatoes, onion, garlic, marjoram, cheese kransky, chorizo, 1L of water, then cover with a lid and bring to boil. Reduce the heat and cook until the carrot and potatoes are soft.
- Add the beans, then stir and slowly pour cornflour mixed with a little bit water to make the soup thicker. Keep stirring, then taste and season with Vegeta gourmet stock. Taste again to see if anything needs to be added.
- Serve on its own and garnish with fresh parsley.

50. Winter Warmer Pumpkin And Turmeric Soup Recipe

Serving: 4 | Prep: 10mins | Cook: 25mins | Ready in: 35mins

Ingredients

- 2 tbs coconut oil
- 3 garlic cloves large minced
- 1/2 onion brown medium
- 1 tbs turmeric root peeled grated
- 1L vegetable stock low salt
- 3 cups butternut pumpkin peeled diced
- 1/2 cup coconut milk
- salt and pepper *to taste

Direction

- In a large saucepan, heat the coconut oil over med-high heat. Cook the garlic and onion until just soft. Add the turmeric and cook for another 3 to 4 minutes.
- Add the stock and the pumpkin, and bring to the boil. Simmer until the pumpkin is tender. Remove from heat and allow to cool slightly.
- Add the cooked pumpkin mixture to a high speed blender. Process until smooth, then add the coconut milk, season with salt and pepper and serve.

Index

A

Almond 3,17

B

Bacon 3,6,19

Barley 3,6

Beef 3,9,10,13

Black pepper 8

Bran 5

Broccoli 3,17

Brussels sprouts 14,15

C

Carrot 3,4

Cashew 3,4

Cauliflower 3,16

Chicken 3,5,6,7,10,11,12,14,15,18,21,22,23,24

Chickpea 3,12,21

Chilli 3,23

Chinese cabbage 4

Chips 3,11

Chorizo 3,19,25

Cinnamon 3,7

Coconut 3,4,7

Coriander 3,23

Couscous 3,7

Cream 3,8

Curry 9,18

D

Dijon mustard 21

E

Egg 3,10

F

Fennel 3,20

G

Gin 3,6,9

H

Ham 3,9,18

Honey 3,5

J

Jelly 4

K

Kale 3,11

L

Lamb 3,7,21

Leek 3,14

Lemon 3,10

M

Matzo 3,12

Meat 3,12

Miso 3,14

Mushroom 3,8

N

Nut 15

O

Oil 3,11

Olive 3,8,11

Onion 3,10

P

Parmesan 24

Pear 3,6,7

Peel 10,22

Potato 3,13,14,22

Pumpkin 3,5,9,14,15,16,17,21,22,25

R

Rice 3,19

S

Salt 8

Soup 1,3,4,5,6,7,8,9,10,11,12,13,14,15,16,17,18,19,20,21,22,23,24,25

Stock 4,6,7,9,10,11,13,14,16,20,21,22,23,24,25

T

Tomato 3,13,23

Turmeric 3,25

V

Vegetables 3,5,22

Vegetarian 3,24

W

Walnut 3,5

Conclusion

Thank you again for downloading this book!

I hope you enjoyed reading about my book!

If you enjoyed this book, please take the time to share your thoughts and post a review on Amazon. It'd be greatly appreciated!

Write me an honest review about the book – I truly value your opinion and thoughts and I will incorporate them into my next book, which is already underway.

Thank you!

If you have any questions, **feel free to contact at:** *author@chardrecipes.com*

Joy Gonzalez

chardrecipes.com

Printed in Great Britain
by Amazon